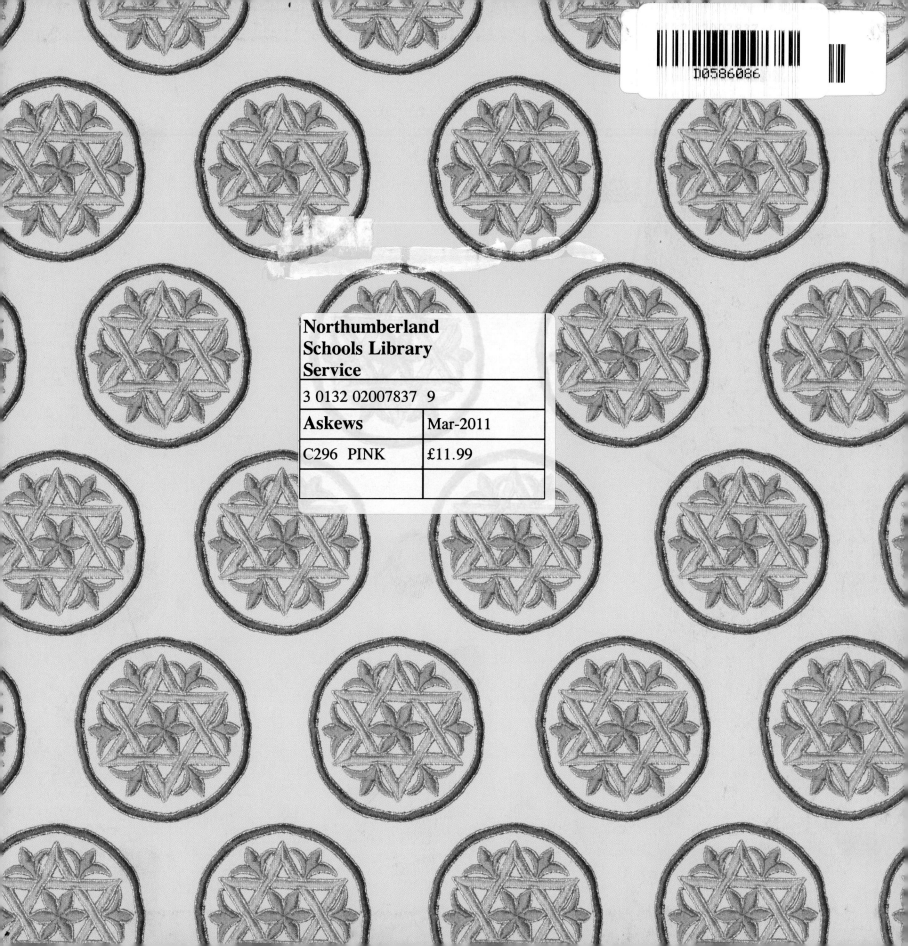

Families and their Faiths—

Judaism in Israel

Written by Frances Hawker and Daniel Taub
Photography by Bruce Campbell

Cherrytree Books

A Cherrytree Book

Published in 2009 by
Cherrytree Books, part of
Evans Publishing Group
2a Portman Mansions
Chiltern Street
London W1U 6NR

British Library in Cataloguing Data
Hawker, Frances
    Judaism in Israel. - (Families and their faiths)
    1. Judaism - Israel - Juvenile literature 2. Israel -
    Religious life and customs - Juvenile literature
    I. Title II. Campbell, Bruce, 1950-
    296'.095694

ISBN: 9781842345443

Editor: Bryony Jones
Designer: Robert Walster, Big Blu Design
Printed in Dubai by Oriental Press

Frances Hawker and Bruce Campbell have travelled all round the world, beginning when they made their way overland from Europe to Australia thirty-five years ago. They have previously published ten children's books together.

Daniel Taub works as an international lawyer and has written a number of books and a television series about Jews and Judaism. He lives in Jerusalem with his wife Zehava, a teacher, and their six children.

Half of the royalties from the sales of this series will go to the local communities featured in the books.

VISIT OUR WEBSITE
Evans
www.evansbooks.co.uk

For more information about the authors and about the people and places featured in this book, please go to our website
www.evansbooks.co.uk

Contents

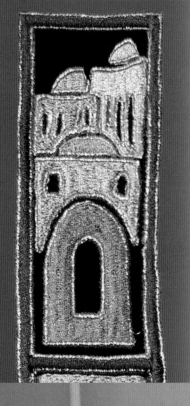

My name is Zvi. Let me tell you a story about one of my grandsons, Asher, and our family. We live in the city of Jerusalem, in Israel.

Asher is nine years old, and loves football. We like to play chess together – he often wins!

Asher has four brothers and one sister. They are all older than him except Amichai, who is four. Here he is on a bike ride with his brothers Reuven and Amichai.

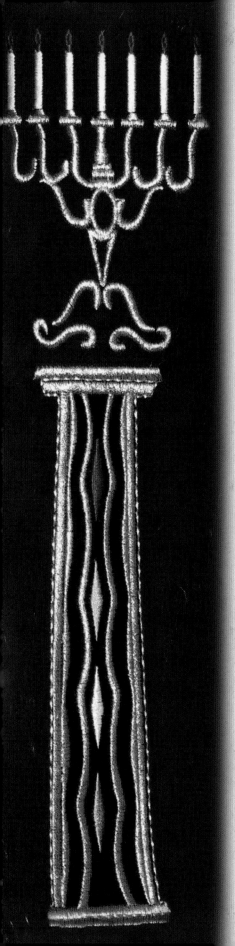

Our family is Jewish. We love celebrations. Have you heard of Passover, Hanukkah or Purim? These are all Jewish festivals. Another celebration is called a Bar Mitzvah, which celebrates a boy's thirteenth birthday. This is a picture of Reuven's Bar Mitzvah. Asher sits on his father's shoulders while everyone else dances!

Asher goes to school every day of the week except Saturday. There are forty boys in his class. The school day starts with prayers at eight o'clock in the morning. He is taught in Hebrew.

At breaktime Asher plays football. Even when he plays sport he wears a hat. This is a sign of respect for God.

It does not matter what kind of hat Asher wears, even his back-to-front baseball cap will do!

Every Friday we get ready for a celebration called Shabbat. Asher and Reuven buy fruit from the market.

Shabbat starts just before sunset on Friday, and ends on Saturday evening. It is our day of rest, so we cannot do any work. No homework or jobs around the house! We spend time with family and friends.

To welcome Shabbat we light a candle for each person in the family.

In the evening we go to our beautiful little synagogue to read from our prayer books and pray. The synagogue is where we worship God.

We remember that God worked for six days to make the whole world. On the seventh day he rested and made this day holy. This is why we rest on Shabbat.

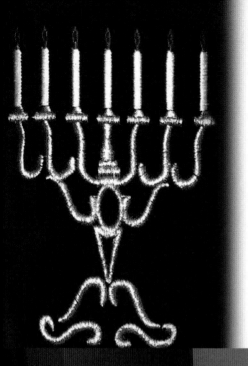

When we get home we have dinner. Asher's father says a blessing and thanks God for the gift of Shabbat. Over dinner we talk, laugh and sing, and at the end of the meal we say grace. Family and friends often visit us for this special dinner.

The next morning we walk to the synagogue for morning prayers. Today is special because Reuven has been asked to read from our holy book, the Torah. This tells the story of the Jewish people, and teaches us how to live.

Shabbat finishes when three stars can be seen in the sky on Saturday evening. Our day of rest is over, and our busy lives begin again straight away. The phone starts ringing for the first time in 24 hours. Asher's mother asks, 'Have you all finished your homework?'

No wonder we look forward to Shabbat each week!

We feel lucky to live in Jerusalem because Jews believe it is the holiest place on earth.

On special days we pray at the Western Wall. Jews come from all around the world to pray here. Reuven straps on his tefillin. These are two little boxes containing prayers. He straps one on his arm near his heart and one to his forehead. They remind him that everything he thinks, feels and does is for God.

Asher is too young to wear the tefillin. He will be able to when he is thirteen and has reached his Bar Mitzvah.

Asher prays and then looks at the hundreds of prayers written on small pieces of paper and stuffed into the cracks between the huge stones. He wonders what everyone has prayed for.

Women also worship here, but in a separate area from the men.

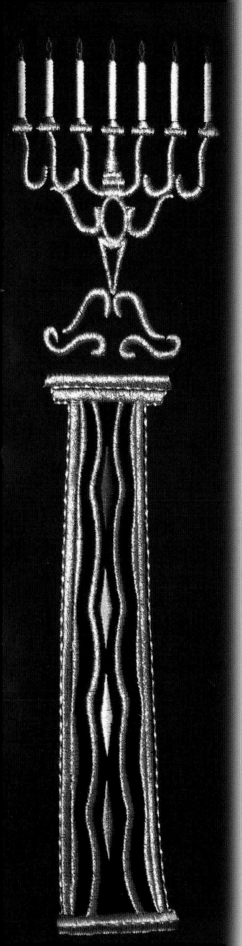

After praying we walk through the old walled city of Jerusalem. Many different people live here, and Asher likes seeing their different clothes and smelling unusual types of food.

We see a group of boys dressed in black and white. Their clothes and haircuts show that they are Jews who have different customs to our family. Many Jewish groups have different traditions, but we are all part of the same people.

Asher's father reminds the boys that Passover will start tomorrow. It lasts seven days, and we celebrate it once a year. We remember how God helped the Jews escape from slavery nearly 3000 years ago.

The night before Passover we search for breadcrumbs by candlelight to make sure there is no bread in the house. During the festival we only eat flat bread called matzah. This reminds us that the Jews left Egypt in such a rush that they didn't have time to let their bread rise.

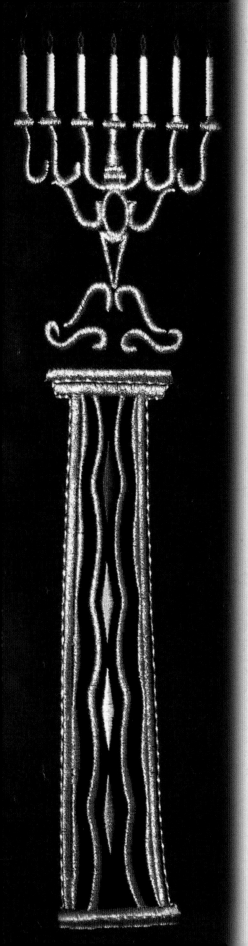

On the first night of the festival we have a special meal called a seder. Amichai asks four questions to find out why this night is so special. The answers remind us that we were once slaves and how important it is to be free.

We eat special foods during the seder. Asher
shudders as he bites into a bitter herb. We laugh
at the look on his face.

'That is to remind you how bitter it is to be a
slave,' his father says.

After Passover ends Asher goes back to school. On Sunday his team plays in the football final. They win!

He shows me his gold medal.
'Well done!' I say. 'I hope you can study the
Torah as well you can kick a football!'

Notes for Parents and Teachers

For more information about the authors and the people and places featured in this book, please go to our website: www.evansbooks.co.uk

Jews follow a religion and way of life called Judaism. Many of its traditions date back 4000 years, and laid the foundations for other faiths like Christianity and Islam. There are some 13.5 million Jews in the world today. While there are different groups and traditions in Judaism, all share the same basic ideals: a belief in one God, a strong feeling of Jewish community, and a commitment to the Torah as a guide to living an ethical and holy life.

The Hebrew word for charity is tzedaka, which literally means 'justice'. In Jewish teaching, giving to those who are less fortunate is not just an act of generosity, but a responsibility of every person. Jews are commanded to give at least ten per cent of what they earn to charity. Asher's family collect money in a charity box.

Page 5

Can you see the tassles hanging out from beneath Asher and Amichai's shirts? These are to remind them of the rules God has asked the Jews to follow.

Pages 6 and 7

The holiday of Hanukkah dates back over 2000 years, to the time when the Syrian emperor Antiochus tried to force the Jewish people to stop practising their religion, and looted their Temple in Jerusalem. Today Jews celebrate the survival of Judaism by lighting the menorah, a seven branched candelabra like that in the ancient Temple.

Purim is a lively carnival festival in which children wear fancy dress and exchange gifts. It celebrates the bravery of the Jewish heroine Esther who prevented a plot to destroy the Jews of Persia.

Bar Mitzvah (for boys) and Bat Mitzvah (for girls) are Hebrew for 'one to whom the commandments apply'. This is the age at which youngsters become responsible for keeping the commandments of Judaism. It happens when girls turn 12 and boys turn 13.

Pages 12 and 13

At the core of Judaism is the Torah, the Hebrew Bible. According to Jewish tradition, the teachings of the Torah were revealed by God to Moses on Mount Sinai.

There are three daily prayers in Judaism - in the morning, afternoon and evening. On Shabbat and at festivals there is an extra service, in remembrance of the extra service on these days in the ancient Temple in Jerusalem.

Since traditional Jews do not drive cars on Shabbat, except in an emergency, they live close to their synagogue.

Page 14

Jews are only allowed to eat food which is kosher. This means only certain types of animals can be eaten (no meat-eating animals or pigs, for example) and these must be killed in a painless way. Jews also do not eat meat and milk foods together, as a sign that life (symbolised by milk) should be kept separate from death (meat).

Pages 18 and 19

The Western Wall is the only remaining wall of the second Temple in Jerusalem which was destroyed 2000 years ago. It is the holiest place in the world for Jews and many boys and girls celebrate their Bar Mitzvah or Bat Mitzvah by visiting it.

Page 23

These Jews are Hassidic Jews, who are part of the Orthodox Jewish movement. Many of them wear long black coats and hats, as seen in the picture.

Pages 26 and 27

Passover takes place in spring, and is the most widely-kept Jewish holiday. The seder meal is a dramatic reenactment of the story of the flight of the Jewish people from ancient Egypt. Jews eat many different foods which recall life in Egypt and sing lively songs throughout the evening.

The four questions that the youngest child asks at the seder are as follows:
1. Why do we eat unleavened bread and not regular bread tonight?
2. Why do we eat bitter herbs tonight?
3. Why do we dip our food into things tonight, but not on any other night?
4. Why do we lean on a cushion while we eat on this night?
To find out the answers, visit www.bbc.co.uk/schools/religion/judaism/passover.shtml.

Page 29

Studying the Torah is one of the most important things Jews are encouraged to do. In addition to the books of the Hebrew Bible, Jews also study the Talmud - an enormous collection of the discussions and stories of the rabbis (Jewish teachers). Some Jews follow the custom of studying one page of the Talmud every day. At this rate it takes them seven years to complete it all!

Glossary

Bar Mitzvah	A Jewish boy's thirteenth birthday, when he becomes responsible for keeping the commandments of the Jewish faith
Blessing	A special prayer said to make an action holy
Hanukkah	A festival on which the menorah, a seven-branched candlestick, is lit
Jerusalem	The capital of Israel and the holiest city for Jews
Matzah	Unleavened (flat) bread eaten on the festival of Passover
Passover	A festival commemorating the freeing of the Jewish slaves from ancient Egypt
Purim	A carnival festival on which children dress up in lively costumes
Seder	A special meal on the first night of Passover
Shabbat	The seventh day of the week, Saturday, on which Jews do no work and spend time with family and friends
Synagogue	A building where Jews meet and pray
Tefillin	Leather boxes containing sections of the Bible worn on the arm and head during morning prayers
Torah	The Hebrew word for the Bible, the Jewish holy book

Index